YOGA KITTENS

RAVETTE PUBLISHING

First published by Ravette Publishing 2012

Ravette Publishing Limited
PO Box 876
Horsham
West Sussex RH12 9GH

ISBN: 978-1-84161-362-8

RANDY

Poetry in motion!

You're only young once!

JERSEY

Take life
one pose at
a time

SKITTLES

Whenever I feel the urge to excercise, I lie down until the feeling passes

LAREDO

Let's stretch

CANDY

Never trust a smiling cat

SNOWSHOES BABY

I don't do conformity

LYRIC

You're only
as young as
your spine
is flexible

SKITTLES

One wrong move and I've only got eight lives left

CANDY

Anything worth doing is worth overdoing

BEBE

What are you looking at?

KAYLA

Shss!
... I'm
meditating

MILES

It's hard to
be humble
when you're
as cute as me

MOLLY

Within a whisker of pawfection

JERSEY

I'm having a catflap!

CHEETO

Other titles available in this series ...

	ISBN	Price
Yoga Dogs - Get in Touch With Your Inner Pup	978-1-84161-357-4	£4.99
Yoga Cats - The Purrfect Workout	978-1-84161-356-7	£4.99
Yoga Puppies - The Ruff Guide to Yoga	978-1-84161-363-5	£4.99

How to order   Please send a cheque/postal order in £ sterling, made payable
to 'Ravette Publishing' for the cover price of the book/s and
allow the following for post & packaging ...

UK & BFPO	70p for the first book & 40p per book thereafter
Europe and Eire	£1.30 for the first book & 70p per book thereafter
Rest of the world	£2.20 for the first book & £1.10 per book thereafter

RAVETTE PUBLISHING LTD
PO Box 876, Horsham, West Sussex RH12 9GH
Tel: 01403 711443   Fax: 01403 711554   Email: ravettepub@aol.com

Prices and availability are subject to change without prior notice.